Learning Through Story

Mathematics

Tricia Kings

Folens
Publishers

Contents

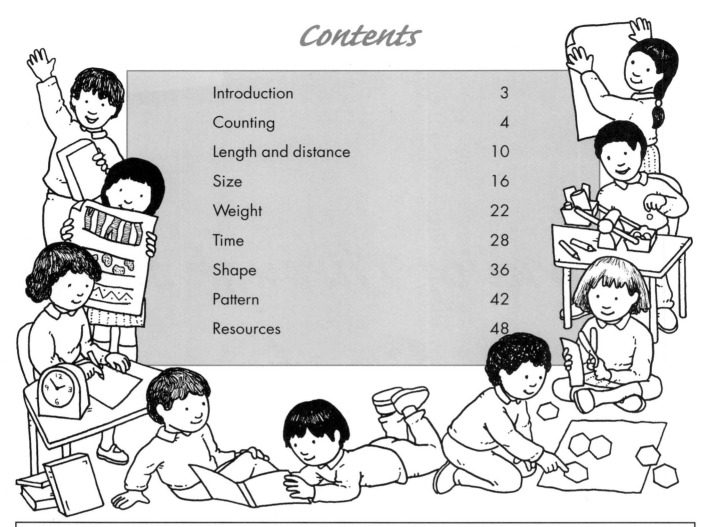

With thanks to Celia Crawford, Will Newman, Rosina Peberdy and Ann Turner.

Editors: Sarah Peutrill and Jane Hammond Foster   Layout artist: Suzanne Ward
Illustrations: Martin Pierce   Cover image: Sue Woollatt – Graham-Cameron Illustration   Cover design: John Hawkins

© 1997 Folens Limited, on behalf of the author.
Every effort has been made to contact copyright holders of material used in this book. If any have been overlooked, we will be pleased to make any necessary arrangements.

British Library Cataloguing in Publication Data. A catalogue record for this book is available from the British Library.

First published 1997 by Folens Limited, Dunstable and Dublin.
Folens Limited, Albert House, Apex Business Centre, Boscombe Road, Dunstable, LU5 4RL, England.

ISBN 1 85276437–6

Printed in Singapore by Craft Print.

Introduction

Learning Through Story – Mathematics provides a collection of ideas and activities based on 43 children's story books. These books have been chosen because of their popularity in schools. Most should be available from school and local libraries and from school lending services.

The use of picture books in a child's curriculum programme both enhances learning and gives the pleasure of enjoying the story itself. Stories provide excellent contexts for many learning experiences – as a springboard to a topic for discussion in the classroom, or as an intrinsic part of the subject work being undertaken.

Each chapter comprises the following elements:

Focus
This details the area of study, key element and learning outcomes of the chapter.

Featured story book
The main thrust of the chapter is developed through one book, appropriate to the teaching of the target concept or skill. It includes discussion and questioning, practical activities and ideas for differentiation so that the teacher can tailor the tasks for children of differing ages and abilities.

Other books
Several extra books are recommended, to develop activities based on the same key area. For each book there are suggested starting points for the teacher to develop in ways that are appropriate for the children they teach.

Copiable activities
At the end of each chapter copiable activities are provided. These can be used either to support the children's learning or as an assessment tool.

Having explored the Mathematics dimension, several of these stories could be developed for use in other curriculum areas.

Out for the Count
Kathryn Cave and Chris Riddell

Tom can't get to sleep, so his mother suggests counting sheep. This is the beginning of a great counting adventure which takes him all the way up to one hundred.

Area of study	Number.
Key element	Counting, groups of ten.
Learning outcomes	Count, order, add, subtract, read and write numbers. Group in tens, ordering tens up to 100. Sort and classify objects. Record and interpret data.

Questions to ask

Why do we have written signs for numbers?

Why is it useful to group in tens?

?

Working with the book

- Have more than one copy of the book available so that children can explore the pictures and text for themselves in pairs, counting and checking the numbers.

- Ask the children: Who likes to sleep with their toys as Tom does? Who has a favourite bedtime toy? Record the data by tallying on a board or large sheet of paper, or in written or graphic form.

- Can the children recall the number of sheep and pirates in the story? Ask them to check their answer with the book.

Who sleeps with toys in bed?

Name	Toys
Philip	Dino
Amarjit	2 teddies
Lucy	Tiger
Kyle	Fluffy

My favourite bedtime toy

Name	Toys
Tom	Rabbit
Dave	Dogger
Dipika	Mrs Bear

LEARNING THROUGH STORY – *Mathematics*

Activities

- Have ready ten toys, or children's drawings of toys cut out and mounted on card – as listed on activity sheet 1. Also prepare ten cards, each with the number 10 written boldly. Choose ten children, one for each toy. Each child in turn holds up their toy and number card, while the rest of the group count aloud: "Ten sheep, ten teddies …", and so on. End with "How many toys altogether? Ten tens".

- Next, say aloud together, "One ten is ten. Two tens are twenty …", while the 'toys' link arms, ending with all ten children linked and a triumphant chorus of "One hundred!"

- Count back by removing one child at a time from the linked line: "Ten tens are one hundred. Nine tens are ninety …".

- Introduce the children to ordinal numbers, using the line of 'toys', saying, "The sheep is number 1; it is the first toy".

Differentiation

- **All children** should be able to count, order, sort, classify, and read and write numbers up to 10.

- **Most children** should be able to explore number patterns for 10, involving multiplication and the '100 square'.

- **Some children** should be able to record and interpret data. Older children could design a board game for younger ones, based on snakes and ladders but using trees and pythons.

One step further

- Look at the page numbers of the book, asking children to find the fifth page or the eighth page and so on.

- Organise a bedtime toy survey with a parallel class or across the whole school. Record findings on a database. What information can be read from such data?

Counting: *Other books to use*

Nine Ducks, Nine
Sarah Hayes

One by one the ducks run away, as all the time a fox gets nearer.

- Ask the children to count back from nine.

- Make nine ducks, number each one and mount them on cane for re-enacting the story, using the information given in the speech bubbles.

- Make number facts about 'nine' using the ducks made above, for example: four children stand with their ducks on one side of the classroom and five on the other. Do this with other combinations.

Over in the Meadow
Louise Voce

As young animals play and make a noise with their mothers in a rural setting, we count up to ten in patterned language and rhyme.

- Count together from one to ten, showing the numbers in figures and then in words.

- Using the pattern of the text, make a communal counting poem about seaside creatures or mini-beasts.

Counting on Frank
Rod Clement

We learn surreal number facts from Frank the dog and the boy who owns him.

- Fill a large and a small jar with sweets or pebbles. Challenge the children to guess how many are in the small jar and then count them – reaching the total by making groups of ten and adding the tens together. Then ask the children to estimate the number in the large jar, before counting these in the same way.

Is there Room on the Bus?
Helen Piers and Hannah Gifford

The intrepid Sam sets off around the world, alone in his bus – but not for long, as alliterative animals fill the bus to bursting point. This is a cumulative story.

● Small groups could make their own lists of ten alliterative animals, for example one old owl, two tame tigers.

First Fairy Tales
Margaret Mayo and Selina Young

An illustrated collection of familiar tales.

● Discuss how the number three often appears in fairy tales, for example three wishes. Encourage the children to spot 'threes' in this and in other stories and transfer them to their own writing.

● Use a number line to count in threes.

Ten in the Bed
Penny Dale

More toys in bed: this time they are rolling over and falling out, one at a time, until the little one is left all alone.

● Groups of ten children can take turns to act and sing this rhyme together, 'falling out of bed' one at a time, until one is left who shouts, "I am cold, I miss you!". The children then join the line one at a time, until there are ten in a bed again!

Using the activity sheets

Activity sheet 1: How many did Tom see?
This sheet is to be used with *Out for the Count*. The children can record the numbers in three different ways – tallying, words and figures.

Activity sheet 2: Hundreds in words
This sheet develops language skills in relation to one hundred.

Name _____

 How many did Tom see?

Sheep		ⅢⅠ II	Seven	7
Wolves		ⅢⅠ ⅢⅠ II	Twelve	12
Pythons				
Goats				
Pirates				
Penguins				
Bears				
Bats				
Ghosts				
Tigers				

LEARNING THROUGH STORY – *Mathematics*

Name _____

Hundreds in words

A century is one hundred years. Here are some more words beginning with 'cent', which are to do with one hundred.

Find out what they mean. Write or draw your answers in the boxes.

Centigrade	Centurion
Cent	Centimetre

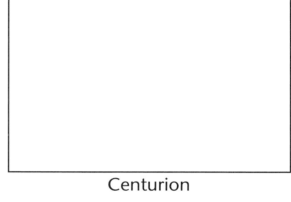

Find a word that begins with 'cent' and is the name for a minibeast with lots of feet. Complete its name and draw a picture of it.

Cent_____

Length and distance

Rosie's Walk
Pat Hutchins

Rosie is a busy, fat, comfortable hen who decides to go for a walk. But Rosie does not realise she is being followed by a fox. Unwittingly Rosie leads the fox into one disaster after another, but arrives home safely herself.

Area of study	Number and measure.
Key element	Length and distance.
Learning outcomes	Use non-standard/standard units of length to measure, estimate and compare.

Questions to ask

How do we usually measure length and distance?

What words do we use to describe length and distance (for example long, short, far, close)?

Are distances the same, whatever our size?

Working with the book

- Discuss the ways that the children could measure the distance Rosie walks. Then complete Activity sheet 3.

- Re-enact Rosie's walk in the playground (using chalk-drawn locations on the ground or objects to represent locations), with children in pairs (one as Rosie walking with little footsteps, one as the fox walking with long paces) while the others count the paces.

- List appropriate measures for length (for example millimetres, centimetres, metres, hand-spans) and for distance (metres, kilometres, paces).

Activities

- Measure and record the length of the classroom using different measures (child paces, teacher paces, metre rule, tape measure, tiles on floor).

- Talk about the difference between standard measures (metres, centimetres) and non-standard measures (steps, hand-spans).

- Ask the children to pace out the length of the hall and record the result. Using a plan of the school, ask the children to look at a selection of distances from their classroom (to the office, to the toilets and so on) and estimate if these distances are longer or shorter than the length of the school hall. Record these estimates and then get the children to check them by pacing out the actual distances. They could record these by drawing a picture of the destination and writing how many paces it is from the classroom.

- Ask the children to pace across the hall and back using the longest strides possible. Record the results. Does the length of their strides relate to their height, length of leg, or length of foot?

One step further

- Using a robot 'turtle' the children could recreate Rosie's walk on the hall floor by programming 'Rosie's steps' or 'fox's footprints' to get Rosie back to her house.

- Children could identify and count the number of different animals on each of the double-page spreads in the book. There are lots of opportunities for counting and observation in the books (for example the number of Rosie's tail feathers, the number of tiers on the beehives).

Length and distance: Other books to use

Ladybird Moves Home
Richard Fowler

When a hungry snail starts eating its way towards Ladybird's leaf, she decides to leave home and find somewhere to live.

- Read the story and follow Ladybird through the book. Ask the children to estimate on which page Ladybird travels the shortest distance.

- Measure the distances on each page with a length of string.

- Ask the children to stick a long piece of string, equal to the total length of Ladybird's journey, on to a piece of paper in a circular shape. They could draw the animals that Ladybird meets next to the appropriate points on the string.

The Great Round The World Balloon Race
Sue Scullard

Miss Fanshawe, Rebecca and William race over deserts, jungles, volcanoes and mountains.

- Using a world map, show the children where each of the competitors started and crashed.

- Ask the children to estimate and then to measure who travelled the furthest and the shortest distances. Record the results and compare the estimates with the actual measurements.

Mrs Smith's Crocodile
Linda Dearsley

Mrs Smith bought a baby crocodile and called him Sweetypie. But Sweetypie grew and grew and why did the local pets start to disappear?

- Challenge the children to estimate how long the crocodile is at each stage by using comparison, for example as long as – a shoe box, a bath, a bed.

- Match in the correct sequence cut-out crocodiles of different lengths with pictures of the animals (and Mrs Smith) that are swallowed.

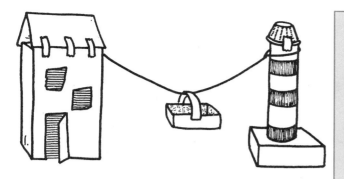

The Lighthouse Keeper's Lunch
Ronda and David Armitage

Every day Mr Grinling rowed out to the lighthouse and Mrs Grinling cooked him a delicious lunch, sent to him in a basket on their own cable system.

- Make a wall plan of the story as a setting, showing the Grinling's house, the coastline and the sea.

- Make a model of the lighthouse to add to the plan, then join the lighthouse to the Grinling's house with a piece of string. Hang a cut-out basket on the string that the children can use to estimate the half-way point between house and lighthouse. Check their estimate by measuring.

- Put the basket in different positions and ask the children to measure how far it is from the house and lighthouse.

Where Are You Going, Emma?
Jean Titherington

Emma is so interested in what she finds on the far side of the orchard that she doesn't notice how far she has wandered.

- Using the playground, or a safe area outside school, measure the distance of a short walk by pacing between landmarks, for example a mark on the ground, a tree and a fence.

- Count how many paces it takes to walk one way, then count how many it takes to run back.

- Record these measurements and draw a plan of the walk.

Using the activity sheets

Activity sheet 3: How many footsteps?
When the children have estimated the longest and shortest distances, ask them to measure them with a 30cm ruler. Ask the children to measure the distances with the 'Rosie' ruler and the 'Foxy Feet' ruler. Then help them to stick cut-out 'Rosie steps' and 'Foxy footsteps' on to a large wall plan of Rosie's walk to show the distances between each place. Using pins show the children how to use string to measure the total length of Rosie's walk. Compare this with the sum of the individual distances measured with the 30cm ruler.

Activity sheet 4: My foot!
The children can work in pairs to draw round each other's feet. They could compare their foot with the teacher's foot, a 30cm ruler, a pencil, a book or a carpet tile.

Name _____

How many footsteps?

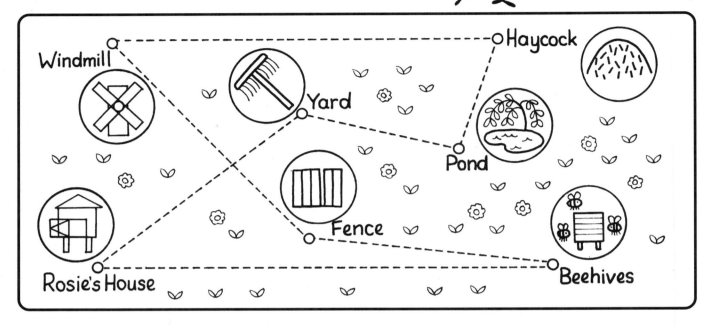

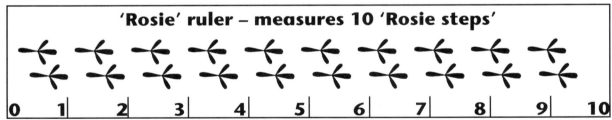

'Rosie' ruler – measures 10 'Rosie steps'

0 1 2 3 4 5 6 7 8 9 10

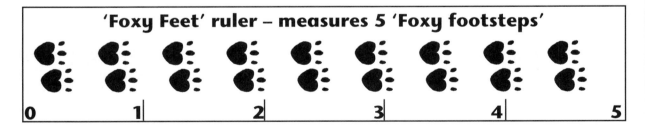

'Foxy Feet' ruler – measures 5 'Foxy footsteps'

0 1 2 3 4 5

Estimate:

- The longest distance Rosie walks.
- The shortest distance Rosie walks.

Cut out the 'Rosie' ruler. Use it to measure the distances and mark them on the plan (for example four Rosie steps between the fence and beehives).

Measure the same distances using the 'Foxy Feet' ruler.

Name _____

My foot!

These are shorter than my foot.

Object	Length in cm

My foot is _____ centimetres long.

These are longer than my foot.

Object	Length in cm

LEARNING THROUGH STORY – *Mathematics*

Size

Jim and the Beanstalk

Raymond Briggs

Jim wakes up to find a beanstalk growing outside his window. At the top, he finds a castle and a very old giant. Jim is able to perform three favours for the giant but then decides he must leave . . . quickly.

Area of study	Size.
Key element	Shape, space and measure.
Learning outcomes	Measure and order objects; use everyday standard and non-standard units to measure, estimate and compare.

Questions to ask

Why do we need to measure someone's size?

What are the different ways we can measure size?

Working with the book

- During the story, encourage the children to identify themselves with Jim – his age and height might be similar to theirs.

- Use the illustrations in the book to encourage the children to estimate how many 'Jims' make a giant.

- After reading the story, find the average height of the children by lining them up and deciding which child comes in the middle. Measure this child in centimetres. Mark this height on a tape on the wall and call this measure the 'Jim'. This will be the 'standard' measure for the following group activities.

- Make a painting of the giant, based on this estimate, making the giant the actual size by using the established 'standard Jim' as a unit of measurement.

Activities

- In the following small-group activities, the children will need to make direct reference to the book, so it would be useful to have more than one copy.

- Allocate one object from the book to each group as in the list shown. The children should compare the sizes of Jim and their object, using language such as 'smaller than' and 'as big as'.

- Ask the children to estimate how many 'Jims' make their object, then measure, using non-standard measures, such as a thumb, a piece of thread or a pencil-sharpener. They can then use the standard 'Jim' measure to find a metric measurement for their object.

- Each group should measure out and make their object, then decide how to display it and write a caption to go with it.

- Make a mural with the life-size giant and all his belongings.

- Ask the children to explain to other classes how the size of the giant and the other objects was decided on.

- Ask the children to draw themselves
  - standing by a giant's foot
  - in a giant's hand
  - talking into a giant's ear
  - trying to eat a giant's sandwich.

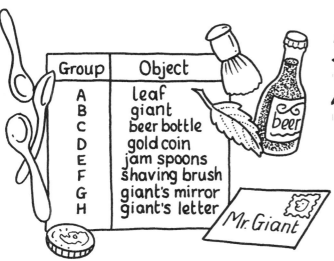

Group	Object
A	leaf
B	giant
C	beer bottle
D	gold coin
E	jam spoons
F	shaving brush
G	giant's mirror
H	giant's letter

Differentiation

- **All children** should be able to compare objects in terms of common, non-standard and standard measures of length.

- **Most children** should be able to use a range of standard units of length with accuracy and confidence.

- **Some children** should begin to understand the concept of scale in measurement.

One step further

- Discuss with the children how you would measure someone for glasses, teeth and a wig.

- Ask the children to draw around their hand on a piece of paper. Show them a jar of beans (for example kidney, butter or broad beans). Ask them to estimate how many beans would be needed just to cover the drawing of their hand. Give them some beans to try it out.

- Show the whole class a drawing of an adult hand. How many beans do they think will be needed to cover this hand?

- Repeat with different-sized beans.

LEARNING THROUGH STORY – Mathematics

Size: **Other books to use**

Tom Thumb
Richard Jesse Watson

The traditional story of Tom, who is as small as a man's thumb.

- Ask the children, if they can, to measure in centimetres the thumb of a man in their family. Compare their findings.

- List all the measurements and show the children how to work out an average measurement. Do they think this is the size of Tom?

- Show the children small objects to give them some idea of Tom's size. For example a thimble, an oak leaf, the head of a thistle, a cherry tomato, a tea cup, a fish bone.

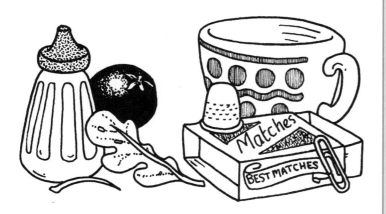

I'm Coming to Get You!
Tony Ross

A hungry monster eats its way through the planets in its own galaxy and then heads for Earth. "I'm coming to get you!" the monster roars at Tommy Brown – but there is a surprise when he pounces ... .

- Discuss the surprise at the end of the book. How big did the children think the monster was, before they got to the last page?

Noah's Ark
Jane Ray

An illustrated version of the story of Noah's ark; the text is an adaptation of the words in the Authorised version of the Bible.

- After reading through the book look particularly at the pages describing the building of the ark. What is the name of the Old Testament unit of measurement used here?

- Use other Old Testament stories, such as 'David and Goliath' to find out about names of Old Testament units of measurement.

Little Penguin
Patrick Benson

Pip is a little Adélie penguin who compares herself in size to the other creatures she meets.

- List all the things in the story that are bigger than Pip.

- Is anything the same size as Pip? If so, what is it?

- What might Pip find that is smaller than her?

The Three Bears and Goldilocks
Jonathan Langley

The traditional story told with humorous text and illustrations.

- Make a chart with three columns headed 'Father Bear', 'Mother Bear' and 'Baby Bear'. Draw all the objects belonging to each bear in the correct size and column.

- Can the children remember what Goldilocks thinks about the size of each object? Write their correct answers on to the chart.

Using the activity sheets

Activity sheet 5: Sizing it up
This requires the children to draw everyday things in proportion to other objects. Discuss each object with children who have more difficulty. Ask them to describe it to you before drawing it. The last part only leaves enough room for the child's face. Help them to realise that the space does not allow them to draw their whole body in relation to the glass.

Activity sheet 6: Higher and longer
This helps to consolidate the children's skills in estimating and measuring.

Name _____

Sizing it up

Draw a pencil that the hand can write with.

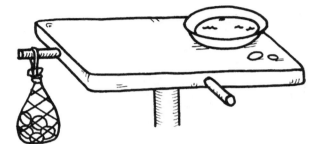

Draw some birds on the bird table.

Draw a remote control handset for the television.

This is a hand puppet. Draw the child's other hand.

Draw a mouse, escaping from the cat.

Draw yourself, drinking the lemonade.

Higher and longer

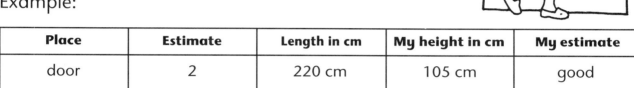

Find four things in your environment that are much higher, or much longer, than you are.

Estimate how many times your height would fit into the height or length of the things that you have chosen.

Check your estimates by measuring.

Example:

Place	Estimate	Length in cm	My height in cm	My estimate
door	2	220 cm	105 cm	good

1

Place	Estimate	Length in cm	My height in cm	My estimate

2

Place	Estimate	Length in cm	My height in cm	My estimate

3

Place	Estimate	Length in cm	My height in cm	My estimate

4

Place	Estimate	Length in cm	My height in cm	My estimate

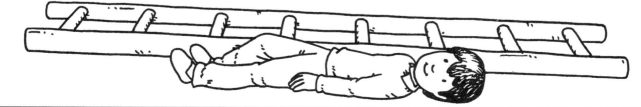

Weight

Who Sank the Boat?
Pamela Allen

Beside the sea live a cow, a donkey, a sheep, a pig and a tiny little mouse. One day they decide to go out in a rowing boat – with disastrous results. This is a lively, rhyming picture book.

Area of study	Weight (mass).
Key element	Shape, space and measure.
Learning outcomes	Understand and use non-standard measures of weight. Estimate and compare.

Questions to ask

How do we know if something is heavy or light?

Are bigger things always heavier?

How do we measure weight?

?

Working with the book

- Before the story, discuss the heaviest and lightest things that the children can think of.

- Read the story and encourage the children to join in with the repetition. Ask:

Do you know who sank the boat?

Was it just the mouse?

What would have happened if the mouse had got in the boat first?

Which animals weigh about the same?

Activities

- Ask the children to balance matching amounts of modelling clay on a balancing scale, then model a cow and a donkey. With other matching amounts they can make a sheep and a pig. Then use a small piece for the mouse.

- Using a tin lid in a bowl of water as a boat, explain how to experiment with different combinations of the modelling clay animals to sink the boat. They should record the animals that sink the boat and then weigh them (in grams). How much weight sinks the boat? (You may need to try this first, to get an idea of what size the animals need to be.)

- Discuss particular times when we weigh things and why we need to know their weight, for example food, babies, holiday suitcases.

- Make a chart of heavy things (weighed in kilograms) and light things (weighed in grams). Ask the children if they think size is always related to weight. Then check this with them by weighing objects of the same size – for example a pencil eraser and a plastic building block – and comparing the weight of each.

- Fill a bag with pennies and another one with polystyrene packing. Ask the children to compare their size and weight.

- Collect pairs of objects and ask the children in groups to decide which they think is the lighter of each pair. If necessary, show them how to check by weighing.

Differentiation

- **All children** should be able to work in groups to identify differences in the weight of objects.

- **Most children** will understand that weight can be measured (non-standard or standard units).

- **Some children** will be able to use scales accurately to record individual weights in grams.

One step further

- Fill a number of jam jars of the same size with a variety of substances, for example sugar, sand, water, marbles.

- Ask the children to put them in order of weight by holding them.

- Then weigh the jars and check against the estimates. Which substance is the heaviest and which is the lightest?

Weight: *Other books to use*

The Lighthouse Keeper's Catastrophe
Ronda and David Armitage

When the keys to the lighthouse are lost Mrs Grinling comes up with a novel idea for getting her husband into the lighthouse.

- Ask some of the children to weigh themselves with bathroom scales and record their weight in kilograms.

- Put a box on the scales for the children to fill with items until it equals their weight.

- Ask them to draw their body shape. Inside this shape they could write or draw the items that equalled their weights.

Mighty Mountain and the Three Strong Women
Irene Hedlund

Champion sumo wrestler Mighty Mountain meets his match when he comes across the three strong women.

- Ask the children to make a list of five things in the book that are lifted or carried (for example a cow, a bucket, a tree). Then place them in order from the heaviest through to the lightest.

How Do You Weigh An Elephant?
Derek Farmer

Nobody can decide how to weigh such a big animal until Chao Chong comes up with an ingenious solution.

- Float a small plastic bowl in a washing-up bowl filled with water. Draw a line around the inside of the plastic bowl, above the water line. The children can experiment with different small items, putting them into the bowl to make the water come up to the line.

LEARNING THROUGH STORY – *Mathematics*

The Shopping Basket
John Burningham

When Steve comes home with his shopping, his basket is not as heavy as it should be because he has used some of the items to trick the animals he meets.

● Using items that might appear in a shopping bag ask the children to estimate which is heaviest by weighing them in their hands. Check with a balance. Record the results.

● Ask the children to fill baskets with similar items and see if they weigh the same.

● Get the children to act as shopkeepers and weigh out amounts of groceries in grams/kilograms.

Using the activity sheets

Activity sheet 7: Sink the boat
Use this sheet for further weighing practice and to give the children an idea of what a kilogram 'feels' like. Provide them with a wide variety of objects that are different sizes to put on the scales.

Activity sheet 8: Estimating and weighing
The children should work in groups, each with balancing scales and a bag of marbles, if possible. They can take it in turns to use the tin lid and bowl of water, the books and the jar. For 'balance the mystery box' create a small box that contains a heavy weight.

Name _____

Sink the boat

1 kilogram of:

It will take a weight of one kilogram to sink this boat.
Put various objects on the scales until they weigh 1 kilogram.
Write the names of the objects you used and draw them inside the
weight shape above.

LEARNING THROUGH STORY – *Mathematics*

Estimating and weighing

How many marbles will it take to...	Estimated number of marbles	Actual number of marbles	Weight of marbles in grams
sink the boat?			
tip the jar?			
balance the books?			
balance the mystery box?			

Estimate how many marbles it will take to complete each task, and write your estimates in the spaces above.

Count and record how many marbles each task actually takes.

Weigh the marbles (in grams) and record the weight each time.

Time

What's the Time, Mr Wolf?

Colin Hawkins

A simple and humorous look at Mr Wolf's day, identifying different times of the day for different activities, with a strong emphasis on meal times, which are very important for Mr Wolf! Different clock faces and his pocket watch clearly show us the time through the day.

Area of study	Time.
Key element	Number and measure.
Learning outcomes	Use standard units of time to measure, estimate and compare.

Questions to ask

Why do we need to tell the time?

Why do we need to know how long it takes to do something?

Working with the book

- Before the story, ask the children if they can tell the time, and whether anyone has a watch. Do they have digital watches or ones with clock faces? Point out all the clock faces in the story.

- Use a large clear clock face (real or model) with moveable hands. For each of Mr Wolf's activities get the children to move the clock's hands to the right time.

- Work out with the children what a digital watch would show for all the times pictured in the story.

- Using both clock face and digital visuals, work out the length of time it takes to do various activities.

Mr Wolf got up at 7:30. He washed and dressed and was ready for breakfast at 8:00.
How long did it take him to get washed and dressed?

Mr Wolf made a cake and put it in the oven at 3:00. At 4:00 it was cooked.
How long did it take to cook?

Mr Wolf went to bed at 9:00, slept all night and woke up at 6:00.
How long was he asleep?

Activities

- Help the children to make a chart with all the important times of their day.

- Work out together a key with symbols for each activity.

- Ask the children to find objects in their home that can tell you the time (for example television, cooker, alarm clock). Make a list and discuss whether each item tells the time verbally or visually or both.

- Play the game 'What time is it, Mr Wolf?'.

- Ask a group of children to tell each other about their favourite time of day. Make sure each child has a chance to tell something to the rest of the group. Is it in the morning, afternoon or evening? Does it last for a short time or a long time?

School day

Time	Activity
7·00	Get up
8·30	Go to school
10·45	Breaktime!

Saturday

Time	Activity
8·00	Get up
9·30	Play football
12·00	Lunch with Grandma

Differentiation

- **All children** should be able to tell the hour of the day from a numbered clock face.

- **Most children** should be able to tell what hour of the day it is from a 12 hour digital watch or clock.

- **Some children** should be able to tell the exact time from both a digital timepiece and a numbered clock face.

One step further

- Using information books, find out and discuss ways in which people measured time in the past, for example sundial, candle clock, egg timer.

- Extend the children's knowledge of time measurement from seconds, minutes, hours and days, into weeks, months and years.

- Look at calendars and how they record days, weeks and months of the year. Discuss how we use calendars to plan our time ahead, for example holidays.

Time: Other books to use

The Stopwatch
David Lloyd

Tom receives a stopwatch from his Gran: now he can time everything!

● Make a list of different activities — such as having lunch, tidying the classroom, running around the playground — and ask the children to predict how long it might take to complete them.

● Ask the children to record the actual time taken for each activity by using a stopwatch. Compare these times with the predictions.

● Demonstrate these results in a bar chart.

Frog and Toad Together
Arnold Lobel

In one of the stories in this book, Frog makes a list of all the things he has to do in the day — and then loses the list.

● Discuss with the children all the things they do in the day. List their answers on the board.

● In groups, look at the list and work out in what order they would do everything through the day.

● When each group has their list in order, get them to put a start time next to each activity. Draw up a timetable for the day, in chart form.

Sunshine
Jan Ormerod

Moonlight
Jan Ormerod

In 'Sunshine' a small girl gets up early, before her mother and father. In 'Moonlight' she takes a long time to fall asleep.

● Discuss the activities in the pictures and the time at which they are taking place.

● Give each child an activity to draw in a sequence of pictures, for example having breakfast or getting dressed.

Peace at Last
Jill Murphy

When the Bear family go to bed there are so many night-time noises that Mr Bear is unable to sleep. In the early morning, back in bed, he nods off to sleep, only to be woken by the alarm clock… .

● Show the children the pictures in sequence, as you read the story.

● Ask them to guess what the time might be at each part of the story. (In some pictures clock faces show the time.)

First Pink Light
Eloise Greenfield

Tyree's father is due back home first thing in the morning. Tyree is determined to stay awake all night so that he can greet his father at the 'first pink light' of dawn.

● Talk about how slowly time seems to pass when you want something to happen — and how quickly it passes when you are enjoying yourself.

● Explain how the 'first pink light' is another way of telling the time. Keep a record, during December and January, of what time it gets light in the morning, and when it gets dark at night.

Using the activity sheets

Activity sheet 9: Telling the time
The children are asked to tick the objects that tell the time just from looking at them. The egg-timer should not be ticked but is intended to provoke discussion. When completed ask the children to look for more ways to tell the time.

Activity sheet 10: Day and night
The children could add symbols to show times for different activities. Some children may need help from a parent or carer.

Activity sheet 11: Time flies
This requires the children to express length of time in minutes and in hours and uses both digital and analogue faces.

Activity sheet 12: Counting the days
Before completing this sheet teach the children the saying: 30 days have September, April, June and November. All the rest have 31, except for February that has 28 days and 29 every leap year .

Name _____

Telling the time

Tick ✔ the objects that tell you the time when you look at them.

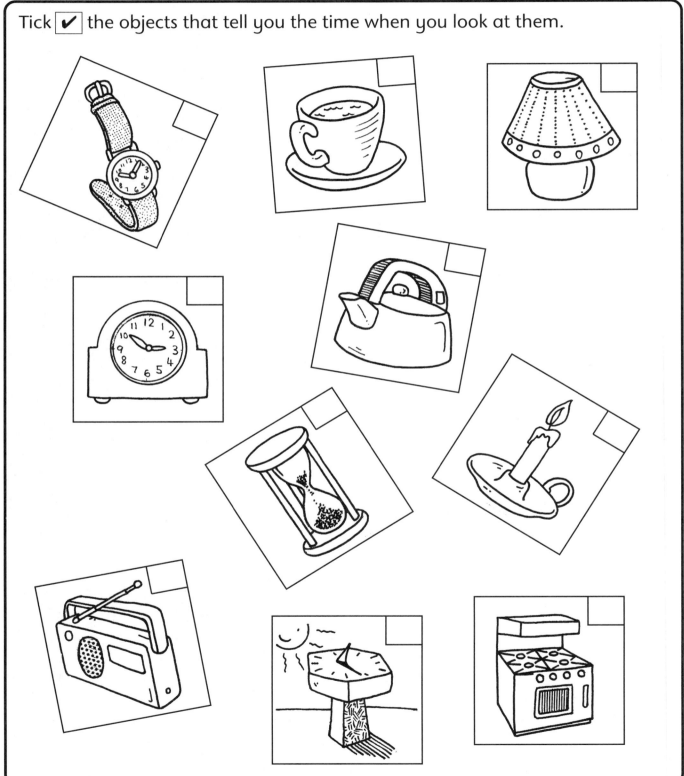

LEARNING THROUGH STORY – *Mathematics*   © Folens (copiable page)

Name _____

Day and night

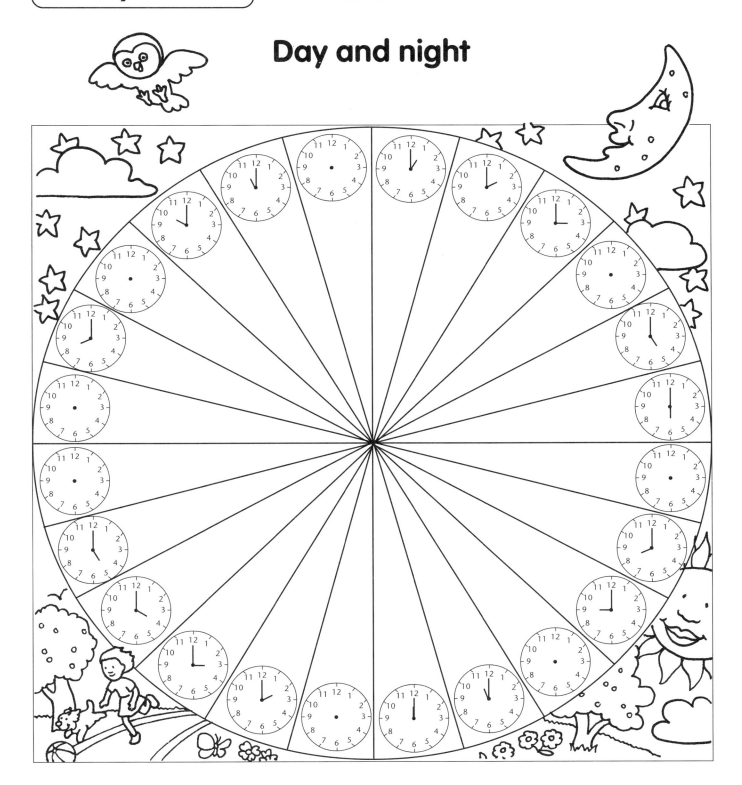

Colour in **blue** all the clocks that show the time when you are asleep at night.
Colour in **yellow** all the clocks that show the time when you are awake
in the day.
Draw in the missing hands on the small clock faces.

Name _____

Time flies

How many minutes does it take Sam to get up and be dressed?

How long does Mary's favourite television programme last?

For how long does Tom read his book?

 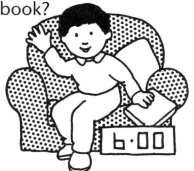 

For how many hours is Mary asleep?

LEARNING THROUGH STORY – *Mathematics*

Name _____

Counting the days

Today is  Helen's birthday is

How many days does Helen have to wait for her birthday?

Helen has to wait _____ days.

Today is  Heena is going on holiday on

How many days does she have to save pocket money?

Heena has _____ days to save.

Today is  Robert's 6th birthday was on

How many days has he been 6?

Robert has been 6 for _____ days.

LEARNING THROUGH STORY – *Mathematics*

Shape

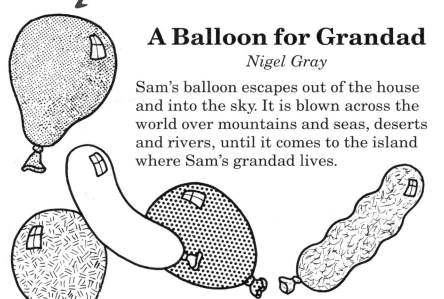

A Balloon for Grandad
Nigel Gray

Sam's balloon escapes out of the house and into the sky. It is blown across the world over mountains and seas, deserts and rivers, until it comes to the island where Sam's grandad lives.

Area of study	Shape, space and measure.
Key element	Geometrical features of shapes.
Learning outcomes	Describe, discuss and sort shapes that can be seen or recognised.

Questions to ask

What different shapes do you know?

Do all shapes have corners and sides?

What simple shapes do we see in our everyday lives?

?

Working with the book

- Look carefully through the book with the children and talk about the pictures. In groups, ask the children what shapes they can find in the pictures. Draw on the board and name a square, a triangle, a circle, a star and an oblong. Have they found all these shapes in the book? Try to have several copies of the book to support group work.

- Talk about which have corners and straight lines and which have curves.

- Discuss natural shapes, and regular and irregular shapes for example, compare a tree to a building.

Activities

- Give the children a list of shapes to find in the school grounds or the locality. Let the children walk around in groups, under supervision, ticking off the shapes as they go. Ask them to do simple drawings of what they see.

- Ask the children to imagine that they are flying high, looking at the earth. What would they see? What sort of shapes would there be? Would they be 2-D or 3-D? (Using cut-out shapes and models, explain to the children the difference between 2-D and 3-D shapes.)

- The children could then work in pairs to do a drawing of what they might see from the air.

- Ask everybody to bring in something for a shape table. Name and label the shapes. Talk about 2-D and 3-D shapes using examples from the table. Working in small groups, ask the children to sort out the shapes in different ways (for example corners/no corners). Have a reporting back session and discuss the sorting criteria with the children.

- Draw five shapes for all the children to see: triangle, circle, pentagon, square and rectangle. Ask the children to draw pictures using these shapes.

One step further

- Discuss further the geometrical features of shapes. Show the children pictures of hexagons, pentagons, cylinders and spheres. Discuss their sides/edges, vertices and surfaces.

- Use the book to develop knowledge of pattern as well as shapes. Look for examples of patterns in the pictures.

Differentiation

- **All children** should recognise and name simple 2-D and 3-D shapes.

- **Most children** should appreciate that some shapes have sides and corners and some have curves.

- **Some children** should begin to understand how 3-D shapes are made up, through using Activity sheet 14.

shape: Other books to use

Granny's Quilt
Penny Ives

Each piece of the quilt tells the story of Granny's life. Her little granddaughter loves to look at the quilt and hear the stories.

- Explain that patchwork quilts use shapes that tessellate. Show some examples.

- Give the children several cut-out circles, squares, triangles and oblongs. Ask them to try to fit the shapes together to make a patchwork pattern. Which shapes work best?

The Ship Shape Shop
Frank Rodgers

Sam and Janet love Salty's Junk Shop – but Mrs Grimbly-Whyte says it is scruffy and wants it demolished. The town council agrees but the day is saved by Granny who comes up with a novel idea to set up the shop in Salty's aged sailing boat.

- Look around the local environment for buildings with unusual shapes and talk about these together.

- The children could draw a picture of a magical place with fantastic buildings, based on all the shapes that they have learned about.

Dear Zoo
Rod Campbell

When I wrote to the zoo asking for a pet they sent all kinds of different animals, in containers of different shapes and sizes.

- Read through the story asking the children to predict what animal is in each container – then lift the flap to see. What other animals might fit in each crate, box or basket?

- Design some funny box houses to suit different shapes of animals on squared paper. Challenge them to make a box for a snake, a giraffe or a hippopotamus. Which box has the most squares?

LEARNING THROUGH STORY – *Mathematics*

The Flyaway Pantaloons
Sue Scullard

A journey over the rooftops of medieval Florence by a pair of pantaloons, with illustrations detailing the shapes of the old buildings.

- Look at the shapes of the buildings and name as many as possible, for example a tower is a cylinder, a steeple is a cone.

- Ask the children to draw examples of these.

Looking Down
Steven Jenkins

This is a wordless picture book that features a tiny ladybird perched on a blade of grass. Seen first from far out in space, in stages the ladybird gets nearer and nearer.

- With the children, look at these pictures of the world seen from above and pick out natural and manufactured shapes.

- Ask the children to draw shapes from above, for example chair, table, cup. Discuss the shapes in these drawings.

The Blue Balloon
Mick Inkpen

A magic blue balloon is blown into some wonderful shapes and colours.

- With a packet of balloons of assorted shapes, ask the children to say what each one will be, for example a flat circular balloon will become a sphere. Then use a balloon pump to blow them up, and check the children's predictions.

Using the activity sheets

Activity sheet 13: Sorting out shapes
This sheet requires the children to find shape in everyday objects. For children who find this difficult, try to provide them with some real examples for them to see and touch.

Activity sheet 14: Shape maker activity
The children can cut out the shapes directly from the sheet or you can enlarge it if you wish to make larger models. Ask the children to think of a use for the finished article: for example the cone could be a pointed hat or a ball-catcher.

LEARNING THROUGH STORY – *Mathematics*

Sorting out shapes

Cut out these pictures and sort them into sets of the same shape.
Say what each shape is, either a **sphere**, **cylinder** or **cuboid**.

sphere   cylinder   cuboid

Shape maker activity

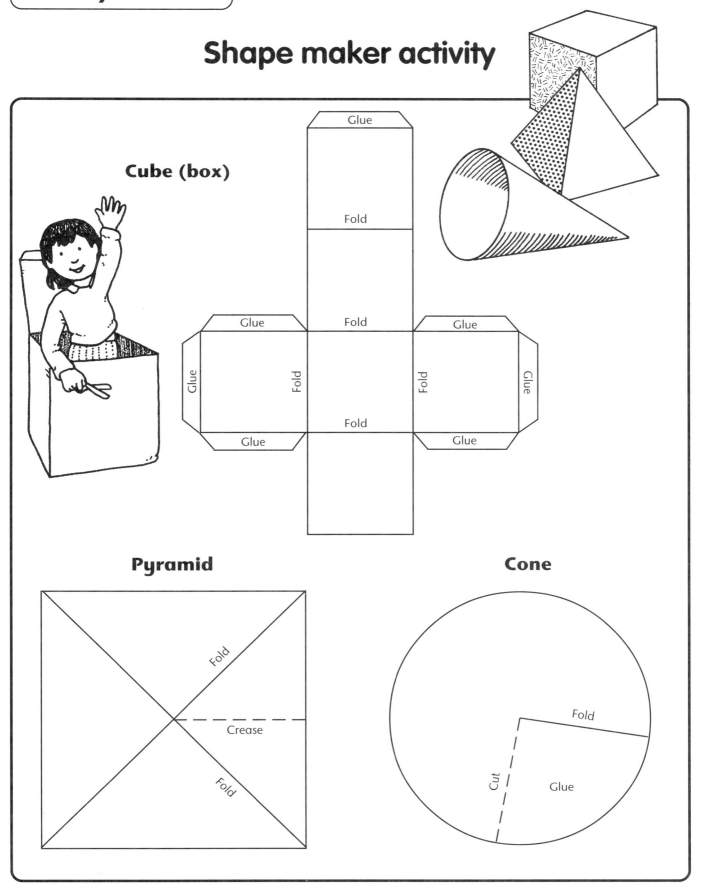

Cube (box)

Glue

Fold

Glue | Fold | Glue

Glue | Fold | Fold | Glue

Fold

Glue | Glue

Pyramid

Fold

Crease

Fold

Cone

Fold

Cut | Glue

Pattern

The Midnight Farm
Reeve Lindbergh

A mother takes her child through the night darkness of the farmhouse and outside to say goodnight to the farm animals, and to the wild animals by the pond.

Area of study	Pattern.
Key element	Shape and space.
Learning outcomes	Describe, discuss and classify patterns, including reflective symmetry, in simple cases.

Questions to ask

What shapes can be used to make patterns?

In what ways can you use shapes to make patterns?

Can you see patterns in nature?

Working with the book

- Look at the first page, especially the patterns on the mother's dress, the border of the curtains and the bedspread. Ask the children to use one shape, repeated many times, to draw a pattern like that on the mother's dress.

- Explain how tessellated patterns are made by fitting lots of the same shapes together without gaps or overlapping. Show them examples from the book. Give small groups of children cut-out squares, triangles or diamonds to make tessellated patterns.

Activities

- Show the children how to make a design by using one shape in different positions, and repeat this design to make a border pattern. Use the children's patterns to make a wall frieze.

- The pattern on the stove on the second page is symmetrical. The children can make a symmetrical pattern by folding and opening out a piece of paper, painting a shape on one side and folding it again. Open it out while the paint is still wet to show the design 'reflected' on the other side.

- Talk about the animal faces in the book, especially the cows, sheep and fox. Are these symmetrical? Cut out large photographs of faces from a magazine. Cut each face in half – then set it next to a mirror so that you can see the whole face again. Is this the same as the original face? What does this tell you about faces?

Differentiation

- **All children** should identify simple shapes, such as a circle, square and triangle, and make patterns by repeating those shapes.

- **Most children** will make tessellated patterns by selecting the appropriate shapes and fitting them together.

- **Some children** will make patterns by rotating shapes and grouping them.

One step further

- Use the book to develop counting skills:

  - Count how many different animals and birds there are in this story.

  - How many are there of each kind of bird and animal?

- Record the data in a chart.

Pattern: Other books to use

The Patchwork Quilt
Valerie Flournoy

Grandma makes a quilt with pieces of different material that bring back memories for all the members of the family.

- Look at how Grandma puts together the pieces for the quilt. Ask each child to bring in a square of material and talk about what it reminds them of. Stick all the pieces together in a patchwork pattern on a sheet of card.

- If possible, show the children an example of a real patchwork quilt and look at illustrations in books for different patchwork patterns and designs.

Greedy Zebra
Mwenye Hadithi

Zebra eats so much and becomes so fat that when the animals are given their coats, Zebra's splits into stripes of black and white.

- Using information books about animals, collect and draw examples of the patterns on the skins, hides and coverings of different creatures, such as the stripes of a tiger or scales of a fish.

Rosie's Walk
Pat Hutchins

Rosie the hen goes for a walk through the farmyard, unaware that she is being closely followed by a fox.

- The pictures in this book use detailed patterns to make them stand out. Ask the children to draw a simple house and garden and then add pattern detail to their drawing.

Elmer
David Mckee

Elmer is a patchwork elephant who likes to play tricks on the other elephants.

● Look at all the decorated elephants at the end of the book, noting the different shapes used to make patterns. Ask the children to design and colour their own decorated elephants.

● Look at the pictures of the trees throughout the book and notice the different shapes and patterns used for the leaves of each tree. Make a big picture for the classroom wall: draw the tree trunks and stick the children's cut-out leaf shapes in each tree, for example triangles on one and circles on another.

● The picture could serve as a background for the children to pin up their patchwork and decorated elephants.

The Prickly Hedgehog
Mark Ezra

Little Hedgehog is lost and looking for his family. When he sees a bunch of spiny chestnuts high up in a tree he mistakes them for his mother, brother and sister.

● This story about the countryside has illustrations of plants and trees with different-shaped leaves. Ask the children to collect different-shaped leaves. Ask them to draw the outline of the leaves and say which are symmetrical.

● Then make leaf prints by placing paper over the leaves and colouring over with crayon to show the pattern of the veins. Again look for symmetry.

Using the activity sheets

Activity sheet 15: Making patterns
This consolidates the children's understanding of simple patterns and symmetry.

Activity sheet 16: More patterns!
This encourages them to look more closely for patterns in the environment.

Name _____

Making patterns

What is this shape?
Draw patterns on another sheet:
- by repeating it
- by turning it round.

Draw the other half
of this pattern so
that it is reflected.

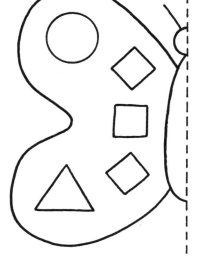

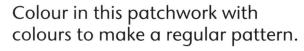

Colour in this patchwork with
colours in any order.

Colour in this patchwork with
colours to make a regular pattern.

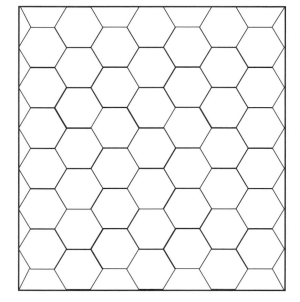

More patterns!

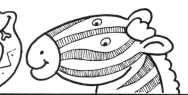

Continue the pattern on each of these:

Crocodile

Snake

Zebra

Find and draw two patterns that you can see on things in your house.

1. Pattern with straight lines:

2. Pattern with curves or circles:

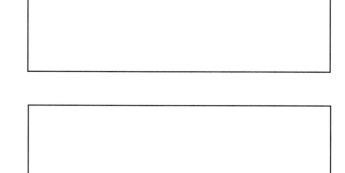

Resources

Counting

Out for the Count by Kathryn Cave and Chris Riddell (Frances Lincoln)

Nine Ducks, Nine by Sarah Hayes (Walker Books)

Over in the Meadow by Louise Voce (Walker Books)

Counting on Frank by Rod Clement (Angus & Robertson)

Is there Room on the Bus? by Helen Piers and Hannah Gifford (Frances Lincoln)

First Fairy Tales by Margaret Mayo and Selina Young (Orchard Books)

Ten in the Bed by Penny Dale (Walker Books)

Length and distance

Rosie's Walk by Pat Hutchins (Picture Puffin)

Ladybird Moves Home by Richard Fowler (Doubleday)

The Great Round The World Balloon Race by Sue Scullard (Macmillan)

Mrs Smith's Crocodile by Linda Dearsley (Simon & Schuster)

Where Are You Going, Emma? by Jean Titherington (Julia Macrae)

The Lighthouse Keeper's Lunch by Ronda and David Armitage (Picture Hippos)

Size

Jim and the Beanstalk by Raymond Briggs (Picture Puffins)

Tom Thumb by Richard Jesse Watson (Picture Puffins)

I'm Coming to Get You! by Tony Ross (Picture Puffins)

Noah's Ark by Jane Ray (Orchard Books)

Little Penguin by Patrick Benson (Walker Books)

The Three Bears and Goldilocks by Jonathan Langley (Picture Lions)

Weight

Who Sank the Boat? by Pamela Allen (Picture Puffins)

The Lighthouse Keeper's Catastrophe by Ronda and David Armitage (Picture Puffins)

How Do You Weigh An Elephant? by Derek Farmer (Longman)

Mighty Mountain and the Three Strong Women by Irene Hedlund (Hippo)

The Shopping Basket by John Burningham (Red Fox)

Time

What's the Time, Mr Wolf? by Colin Hawkins (Little Mammoth)

The Stopwatch by David Lloyd (Walker Books)

Frog and Toad Together by Arnold Lobel (Mammoth)

Sunshine by Jan Ormerod (Picture Puffins)

Moonlight by Jan Ormerod (Picture Puffins)

Peace at Last by Jill Murphy (Macmillan)

First Pink Light by Eloise Greenfield (Black Butterfly)

Shape

A Balloon for Grandad by Nigel Gray (Orchard)

Granny's Quilt by Penny Ives (Hamish Hamilton)

The Ship Shape Shop by Frank Rodgers (Picture Puffins)

Dear Zoo by Rod Campbell (Picture Puffins)

The Flyaway Pantaloons by Sue Scullard (Macmillan)

The Blue Balloon by Mick Inkpen (Picture Knight)

Looking Down by Steven Jenkins (Houghton Mifflin)

Pattern

The Midnight Farm by Reeve Lindbergh (Picture Puffins)

The Patchwork Quilt by Valerie Flournoy (Picture Puffins)

Greedy Zebra by Mwenye Hadithi (Picture Knight)

Rosie's Walk by Pat Hutchins (Picture Puffins)

Elmer by David Mckee (Red Fox)

The Prickly Hedgehog by Mark Ezra (Magi Books)

LEARNING THROUGH STORY – *Mathematics*